MISSION: SPACE SCIENCE

EARTH AND THE MOON

Sarah Eason

Use Your STEM Skills to Explore Our World and Moon

CHERITON
CHILDREN'S BOOKS

Published in 2025 by **Cheriton Children's Books**
1 Bank Drive West, Shrewsbury, Shropshire, SY3 9DJ

Copyright 2025 Cheriton Children's Books

First Edition

Author: Sarah Eason
Designers: Paul Myerscough and Steve Mead
Editor: Jennifer Sanderson
Proofreader: Ella Newby
Consultant: David Hawksett, BSc

Picture credits: Cover: Shutterstock/Rawpixel.com (t), Shutterstock/Evgeniyqw (b). Inside: p4: Shutterstock/Triff, p5: Shutterstock/Solcan Design, p6b: Shutterstock/Digital Storm, p6t: Shutterstock/Sander van der Werf, p8: Shutterstock/Brandpunkt, p9: Shutterstock/Yevhenii Chulovskyi, p10: Shutterstock/Klagyivik Viktor, p11: Shutterstock/Boivin Nicolas, p12: Shutterstock/Krivosheev Vitaly, p13: Shutterstock/Zef Art, p14: Shutterstock/Stefania Valvola, p15: NASA/JSC, p16: NASA/MSFC, p17: NASA/JSC, p18: NASA/JSC, p19: NASA/Neil A. Armstrong, p20: NASA/JSC, p21: NASA/JSC, p22: NASA/JSC, p23: CSNA/Siyu Zhang/Kevin M. Gill, p24: Shutterstock/Siberian Art, p25: NASA/Lunar Receiving Laboratory, p26: Wikimedia Commons/Justus Sustermans, p27: NASA/JSC, p28: NASA, p29: NASA/ARC, p30: Shutterstock/Dima Zel, p31: Shutterstock/Mopic, p32: Shutterstock/Lukasz Pawel, Szczepanski, p33: NASA/Goddard/Arizona State University, p34b: Shutterstock/Bluestork, p34t: Shutterstock/Dima Zel, p35: Shutterstock/Siberian Art, p36: NASA/Michael DeMocker, p37: NASA/Aubrey Gemignani, p38: NASA/Ames, p39: Shutterstock/Mechanik, p40: NASA/SpaceX, p41: NASA/JSC, p42-43: NASA, p44: NASA/JSC, p45: Shutterstock/Supamotionstock.com.

All rights reserved. No part of this book may be reproduced in any form without permission of the publisher, except by a reviewer.

Printed in China

Please visit our website,
www.cheritonchildrensbooks.com
to see more of our high-quality books.

CONTENTS

Chapter 1

AMAZING EARTH

Earth is an amazing place. Our planet is covered with lush rain forests, craggy mountains, deep seas, and frozen ice caps. Most places on the planet are teeming with life, from the tiniest bacteria to the tallest trees—and, of course, humans, too. We are so used to Earth and its wonders that sometimes it is hard to remember that Earth is just one of the billions of planets scattered throughout the universe.

A Rocky Planet

Not all planets are created equally. Earth is a rocky planet like Mercury, Venus, and Mars. Many larger planets (including Jupiter and Saturn) are made of liquid and gas, with no solid surface. Earth has a hard crust that surrounds it. Compared with the other layers of Earth, the crust is extremely thin: it is only about 20 to 30 miles (32 to 48 km) thick on land and 3 to 6 miles (4.8 to 9.6 km) thick beneath the oceans. Beneath the planet's crust there is a dense mantle of hot rock that can behave like a thick liquid. At the center is an iron core that is solid in the middle but liquid where it meets the mantle.

From space, Earth's enormous oceans, vast areas of lush rain forest, great mountains, and ice caps can all be seen.

A Great, Big Jigsaw

Earth's crust is broken up into large chunks called tectonic plates, a little like a giant jigsaw puzzle. These plates "float" on top of the mushy mantle, and although they move very slowly, their edges are constantly bumping and rubbing against each other. Where this happens, earthquakes and volcanoes are common. In some places, the plates are being pushed together, and in other places, they are moving apart.

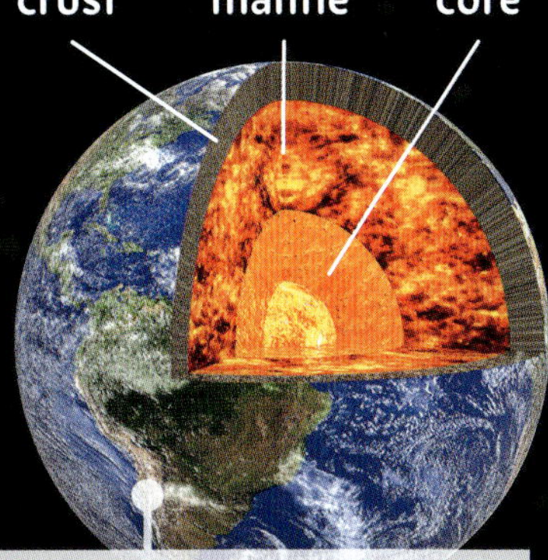

This cutaway diagram shows Earth's layers, including the hot rock of its mantle and core.

SPACE SCIENCE

No one has ever been beneath Earth's crust. The deepest hole ever drilled went only about 7.6 miles (12.2 km) into Earth's crust—about 25 to 30 percent of the way to the mantle. So how do we know what is below the crust? One method for figuring it out is by studying the way that seismic waves from earthquakes travel through Earth. The waves travel at different speeds, depending on the material that they are traveling through, and measuring them helps scientists make predictions about what lies beneath the crust.

YOUR MISSION

In this book we will explore Earth and the moon in detail, looking at what we know about them and how we learned it. You will also be given thought-provoking space missions to complete that will draw on:

- Your STEM skills: these are science, technology, engineering, and math skills.
- Your social skills: these include identifying skills and strengths in others, team building, persuasive skills, and learning how to work collaboratively.
- Your critical thinking skills: these include being able to evaluate and analyze information, think independently about problems and find solutions, and draw your own conclusions.

All the above skills are vital for successful space exploration—ask any space scientist! So, are you mission-ready? Let's begin the missions and find out.

Earth's atmosphere protects us from some of the sun's harmful radiation. It also traps the sun's heat, keeping Earth's temperature fairly consistent.

A Special Atmosphere

One thing that makes Earth so special is its atmosphere, made up of a mixture of gases that surround the planet like a blanket. Without the atmosphere, life could not exist—it contains the oxygen that humans and other animals need to breathe, as well as the carbon dioxide that most plants need to make food.

Weather and Protection

The atmosphere is also responsible for our weather, and it helps protect the surface from meteorite impacts and other space objects. Its only downside is that it obscures our view of outer space, which is why we launch telescopes into orbit, where they have a clearer view.

What Is the Atmosphere Made Of?

The atmosphere is about 300 miles (482 km) thick, but most of the mass in it is within about 10 miles (16 km) of the surface. The farther up you go, the thinner the atmosphere becomes. Most of the matter—about 78 percent—is nitrogen. Oxygen makes up 21 percent of the atmosphere, and argon, carbon dioxide, water vapor, and other gases make up the remaining 1 percent.

Important Levels

Earth's atmosphere is divided into five main layers. Closest to the surface is the troposphere. It is about 4 to 12 miles (6.4 to 19.3 km) thick, and it is where most of our weather takes place. Above that layer is the stratosphere, where jet airplanes fly. Combined with the mesosphere, it forms the middle atmosphere. Above this level are the thermosphere and the exosphere. Scientists use many different methods to study the atmosphere, including weather stations, radar, satellites, weather balloons, and other tools.

SPACE SCIENCE

We are lucky to have our atmosphere. The planet Mercury has almost no atmosphere at all, leaving it unprotected. Mercury's surface is pockmarked with craters caused by objects crashing into it. With no atmosphere to redistribute heat, the planet is boiling hot during the day and freezing at night. Mars also has a very thin atmosphere, leading to similar problems. Although there is frozen water in its crust, the lack of atmospheric pressure means that it cannot have liquid water on the surface.

Stealth fighter planes like this one fly in the stratosphere, the middle section of Earth's atmosphere.

Magnetic Protection

It is not just the atmosphere that surrounds Earth. Our planet's magnetic field cannot be seen or touched, but it plays just as important a role in protecting life on Earth. It is like a giant force field that protects the planet from the sun's radiation. The sun emits a stream of charged particles called the solar wind that travels out into the solar system. Earth's magnetosphere deflects the solar wind and protects the planet. If Earth did not have it, things would be very different. For example, Mars's magnetic field is so weak that it cannot prevent the solar wind from gradually stripping away the planet's atmosphere.

Made in the Core

Scientists believe that Earth's magnetic field is generated by movements in the liquid part of the planet's core. The inner and outer core spin at different rates, and this creates what is called the dynamo effect, causing Earth to behave like a huge electromagnet. Like a magnet, it has two poles: north and south.

This diagram shows how Earth's magnetosphere surrounds the planet, protecting it from the solar winds that travel from the sun.

The Northern Lights are eerily spectacular displays of color that can be seen in the planet's northernmost regions.

Moving Poles

Earth has a north and south pole at the ends of Earth's axis, the imaginary line that goes through the center of the planet. However, the magnetic north and south poles are not located along Earth's axis. They do not stay in one place, either—they "wander" by about 25 miles (40 km) per year. Once in a long while, the poles flip; the last time this happened was 780,000 years ago. Sometimes, large earthquakes can also change the magnetic field. Scientists are still trying to figure out exactly how changes deep within Earth can affect the planet's magnetic field.

SPACE SCIENCE

From time to time, shimmering lights illuminate the areas in the far north and far south of the planet. These are the auroras, also known as the Northern Lights or Southern Lights. Long ago, the Vikings believed that the aurora was a fiery bridge to the sky, built by the gods. Scientists now know that the auroras are caused when particles of the solar wind hit Earth. The particles interact with Earth's magnetosphere and atmosphere, causing the brilliantly colored lights.

YOUR MISSION

If you were in charge of a mission to find another habitable planet, what would be the key factors you would search for to determine if human life could survive? Consider what you have learned so far about Earth and why its conditions encourage life.

Chapter 2

MYSTERIES OF THE MOON

Aside from the sun, the moon is the biggest and brightest object in the sky. For thousands of years, early peoples watched the moon, marking the passage of time as it waxed and waned. It takes about 29.5 days for the moon to complete one orbit of Earth, and this formed the basis of many early calendars—the English word for "month" comes from "moon." Although the modern Western, or Gregorian, calendar does not strictly follow the lunar cycle, some calendar systems, including the Islamic calendar, do.

A Goddess Moon

Many early cultures linked the moon with a god or goddess. For the ancient Greeks, the moon represented Artemis, the twin sister of Apollo. She was also the goddess of the hunt and she had a fierce temper. For the Fon people of Benin, the goddess Mawu represented the moon. She was also the goddess of night, joy, and motherhood.

A full moon in the fall is often called a "Harvest Moon." This is because farmers can stay out late, harvesting their crops by its light.

Stories about the Moon

In some cultures, stories about the moon are told to explain its behavior. For example, the Inuit of North America saw the sun and moon as brother and sister. The god Anningan was the moon, and the goddess Malina was the sun. Every month, Anningan became thinner and thinner as he chased Malina across the sky, forgetting to eat. Then, during the new moon, he disappeared to eat before returning to start the chase again. Malina wanted to evade her brother so the moon and sun would rise and set at different times.

This carving of a moon goddess comes from the Dominican Republic, in the Caribbean.

SPACE HISTORY

The full moon is given many different names throughout the year. The Algonquian peoples of North America had a different name linked to nature and the seasons for the full moon each month. For example, June's moon was the "Strawberry Moon," because strawberries were ready to be picked, and November was the "Beaver Moon," because it was time to set beaver traps before the swamps froze.

The moon affects the tidal movements of Earth's oceans. This action probably seemed very mysterious to ancient people.

Inspiring Stories and Legends

Throughout history, the moon has inspired many stories and legends. Many of them are based on the idea that the moon can affect events and people's behavior on Earth. For example, many cultures associate the full moon with unusual or dangerous behavior, such as sleepwalking and committing suicide or violent acts.

The Moon and Madness

Doctors and other professionals really believed that there was a strong link between madness and the full moon. In eighteenth-century England, people on trial for murder were sometimes given a lesser sentence if the crime happened during a full moon, the idea being that the moon made them do it. Language is related to the moon, too. Our words "lunatic" and "lunacy" come from Luna, who was the Roman goddess of the moon.

Links to the Weather

There are many beliefs and superstitions linking the moon to weather on Earth. For example, one widespread belief is that when a new moon falls on Monday, good weather will follow. Another is that a reddish moon predicts wind. Although the moon does cause tides, its effects upon the weather are actually relatively small.

The Lunar Cycle

People have suggested that the moon's gravity, which pulls on Earth's oceans and causes tides, has a similar effect on the liquids in our bodies. During a full moon, they say that pull is strongest, causing a change in people's behavior. The pull of the moon's gravity increases only when the moon is closer than usual to Earth, and that occurs each month as the moon's orbit around Earth is not a perfect circle. There is no scientific evidence to show that crime figures or other statistics go up and down along with the lunar cycle.

Space History

Many cultures tell stories about werewolves—people who turn into dangerous part-wolf creatures after being bitten by one. Some of the most famous stories involve the person transforming into a werewolf during the full moon, which is probably based on the beliefs linking the full moon to violence and madness. Some legends of werewolves are ancient. In most of the older stories, the werewolf transformation is triggered by things other than the moon.

In many stories about werewolves, people turn into the part-wolf monsters during a full moon.

Pythagoras was an extraordinary scientist who studied the night sky in ancient Greece, long before telescopes were available.

Science and the Moon

In addition to all the myths and superstitions, thousands of years ago, there were also people studying the moon from a scientific perspective. The writings of the Greek astronomer Pythagoras (c. 570–c. 495 BCE) show that he understood that the moon was spherical. He also believed that the moon orbits Earth—though at the time, most people thought that everything revolved around Earth.

Studying the Moon

Another Greek, Aristarchus of Samos (c. 310–c. 230 BCE), was able to estimate the size of the moon in 270 BCE, based on the amount of time that it spends in Earth's shadow. He estimated it at 0.33 of Earth's diameter, which is not far off the actual figure of 0.27. Other ancient astronomers were able to track the moon's position so accurately that they could predict both solar and lunar eclipses.

Making Maps

Once telescopes were invented in the early seventeenth century, people were able to learn more about the moon. Galileo Galilei (1564–1642) used his telescope to make detailed drawings of the moon's surface. As telescopes improved, the maps improved. Two German astronomers were able to use math to calculate the height of many of the moon's mountains in the 1830s.

The Cause of Craters

Mountains and valleys were easy to understand because they were similar to geographical features on Earth. However, craters were a different matter, and no one knew what caused them. Galileo thought that they were volcanic, and other theories included circular glaciers and coral atolls. It was only in the twentieth century that they were proven to be caused by impacts from other objects.

Craters on the moon's surface fascinated early astronomers, who had many different theories about what had caused them.

SPACE HISTORY

Before telescopes were invented, no one was quite sure what the light and dark patches on the moon were. The writings of Aristotle (384–322 BCE), which were widely believed, stated that all heavenly bodies were perfect spheres, so the idea that the markings were mountains and valleys went against this. Some people suggested that the moon acted like a giant mirror, reflecting shapes on Earth. Once telescopes were available for studying the moon, it became clear that it did actually have mountains, craters, and valleys.

YOUR MISSION

Imagine you are on a mission to find new planets. You must report back on discovering these new worlds, detailing their landscapes. Consider that we are aware of features such as mountains, craters, and valleys because we have seen them on Earth, but different formations could exist on other planets. If features other than those found on Earth exist, what might they be like and what factors could influence their shape and form?

Chapter 3

MISSION TO THE MOON

In the 1950s, the United States and the Soviet Union were locked in what is known as the Cold War. This conflict was not a war waged with weapons, but rather an intense competition between two different cultures: the capitalism of the United States and the communism of the Soviet Union. Each country turned to science to prove that its way was best, and billions of government dollars were pumped into scientific research, including space travel.

Flights to the Moon

Early attempts to reach the moon were unsuccessful. The National Aeronautics and Space Administration's (NASA's) Pioneer program and the Soviet Union's Luna program both experienced several launch failures. Finally, in 1959, Luna 1 flew within about 3,700 miles (5,955 km) of the moon. That same year, Luna 2 became the first humanmade object to land on another body in the solar system. Later that year, Luna 3 sent back the first images of the far side of the moon, which is never visible from Earth.

A launch vehicle called Juno II carried the Pioneer 4 satellite into space on March 3, 1959 (see opposite). The spacecraft passed the moon, then went into orbit around the sun.

Planning Manned Missions

Meanwhile, with the exception of Pioneer 4, which reached a point about 37,300 miles (60,000 km) from the moon, NASA's spacecraft were failing one after the other. Finally, they began to catch up. In 1964 and 1965, three successful Ranger probes sent back thousands of images of the lunar surface. NASA scientists used these in their planning for manned missions.

Orbit Successes

In 1966, the Soviet Union achieved another first when it successfully put Luna 10 into orbit around the moon. NASA's Lunar Orbiter 1 was only a few months behind. Mastering this technique was crucial, because any crewed mission to the moon would require an orbiting spacecraft.

Space Science

In order to design a spacecraft that could safely land humans on the moon, scientists needed more than just images—they needed detailed data about the moon's surface. For example, they needed to know if a lander would sink into the dust on the surface, or break through the crust. In 1966, Luna 9 achieved the first soft landing on the moon, and NASA's Surveyor 1 managed it just four months later. Earlier spacecraft had been destroyed when they crashed into the moon, but these soft landers survived the landing and sent back extremely useful data.

The unmanned Surveyor 3 spacecraft was successfully deposited on the moon in 1967, to explore its surface.

Learning Much

The early unmanned spacecraft increased our knowledge about the moon. For example, they sent back data about interplanetary gases, radiation levels on the moon, and its weak magnetic field. However, one of their main objectives was to help scientists prepare for a crewed mission to the moon. For example, from its position in orbit around the moon, Lunar Orbiter 1 sent back high-quality images of several potential landing sites. Other spacecraft, both US and Soviet, analyzed the soil and tested it for radioactivity.

The Apollo 8 spacecraft was launched from Kennedy Space Center in 1968, carrying a team of astronauts to the moon.

SPACE SCIENCE

In 1967, NASA's Surveyor 6 spacecraft successfully landed on the moon. After it touched down, its engines were fired to lift it about 10 feet (3 m) off the surface and then touchdown a few feet away. Then it took images of its original landing site, looking to see if its rockets' exhaust had created a crater. There was no crater, which meant that the moon's surface must be solid and therefore—hopefully!—safe for astronauts to land on.

This famous image captures the moment that Buzz Adrin walked on the surface of the moon.

Heroes on the Moon

The Apollo 11 astronauts stayed on the moon's surface for about 21 hours. During that time, they deployed a solar-powered device containing a set of scientific instruments. The device could measure seismic activity and properties of the surface. The astronauts also collected rock samples to take home for analysis. When they landed back on Earth, they were greeted as heroes.

The Apollo 14 Lunar Module on the moon, with the US flag placed on its surface.

Five More Missions

Five additional crewed missions landed on the moon. Like Apollo 11, each one consisted of a Command Module manned by one astronaut, which remained in orbit, and a Lunar Module crewed by two astronauts, which landed on the surface to explore and conduct experiments. The Apollo 12 astronauts collected samples and took readings of the solar wind, the magnetic field, and the atmosphere. They also visited the Surveyor 3 spacecraft, which had made a soft landing two years before. They brought back some of its parts to examine on Earth.

Here, astronaut and pilot Harrison H. Schmitt is photographed next to an enormous boulder on the surface of the moon. The photograph was taken during the Apollo 17 mission.

Last Journeys

Apollo 13, in 1970, was nearly a disaster. An onboard explosion made the astronauts abort the mission, but they managed to return safely to Earth. After a gap of nine months, Apollo 14 successfully landed on the moon. Apollo 15 made history by bringing along a Lunar Roving Vehicle (LRV), which the astronauts could drive across the lunar terrain. This allowed them to cover a much wider area during the time they had on the moon. Apollo 16 and 17 followed in 1972, each with their own LRV and set of scientific tools. Since then, no one has visited the moon.

SPACE SCIENCE

Although the Soviet Union never succeeded in landing a cosmonaut on the moon, it did continue to bring back new data. In the 1970s, three Luna spacecraft were able to return samples of moon rocks and dust to Earth. They also sent two successful robot rovers to explore the moon's surface: Lunokhod 1 in 1970 and Lunokhod 2 in 1973. The first traveled more than 6 miles (9.6 km) and sent back 20,000 images. The second covered about four times the distance and took four times as many images.

Looking Elsewhere

After the Apollo missions, interest in the moon waned, and scientists turned to other areas of research. Sending humans to the moon was expensive and dangerous, and there was a limit to how much they could learn. There were other exciting things to learn by studying other bodies in the solar system, as well as developing Earth-orbiting space stations such as Skylab, and new forms of transportation such as the space shuttle.

This close-up view of the Skylab space station shows it in orbit around Earth, seen below.

More Moon Missions

Today, there is a huge resurgence in lunar exploration and improved technology means that we can learn more about it than the Apollo astronauts could. In 1990, the Japanese Hiten spacecraft entered orbit around the moon, where it tested out various technologies. In the late 1990s, NASA's Lunar Prospector probe orbited the moon to search for water ice and other minerals. It was also able to map the composition of the moon's surface. The European Space Agency (ESA) launched its first lunar orbiter in 2003.

Moon Discoveries

The Japanese Aerospace Exploration Agency (JAXA) launched Kayuga in 2007. Its tools included a high-definition television camera for sending back crystal-clear images, as well as a variety of other tools. China entered the field with Chang'e 1 in 2007. This spacecraft was able to create a highly accurate three-dimensional (3-D) map of the lunar surface, as well as analyze the chemical makeup of the surface. It also studied the impact of solar activity on Earth and the moon. Recent and current missions have discovered water ice on the moon, as well as some unbelievably cold areas in deep craters.

SPACE SCIENCE

In the 1950s and 1960s, space exploration was dominated by the United States and the Soviet Union. However, exploring the moon—and the rest of space—is now a truly international endeavor. For the past several decades, ESA has been bringing together the top space scientists from around Europe, and JAXA has been conducting its own research. India's Chandrayaan-1 spacecraft, consisting of an orbiter and lander, successfully studied the moon in 2008 and 2009. India's Chandrayaan-3 became the first probe to land near the moon's south pole in 2023.

The Chang'e-4 lander was launched on December 7, 2018. It is shown here on the surface of the moon.

YOUR MISSION

Your mission is to carry out a collaborative exploration of space, working with people from around the world. All team members will work on board the same spacecraft. You are responsible for ensuring that team members work together without any problems. How will you ensure the mission is successful? Consider the following:

- Cultural differences
- Language differences
- Training differences

How would you accommodate the above to make sure the team works effectively?

Chapter 4

LEARNING MORE

Decades of study with telescopes, probes, and crewed missions have meant that we probably know more about the moon than we do about any other object in space. We know, for example, that it is made up of concentric layers, similar to Earth. The rocky outer crust is about 40 miles (64 km) deep, and below that there is a mantle about 620 miles (1,000 km) thick. At the center is a metallic core less than 217 miles (350 km) wide.

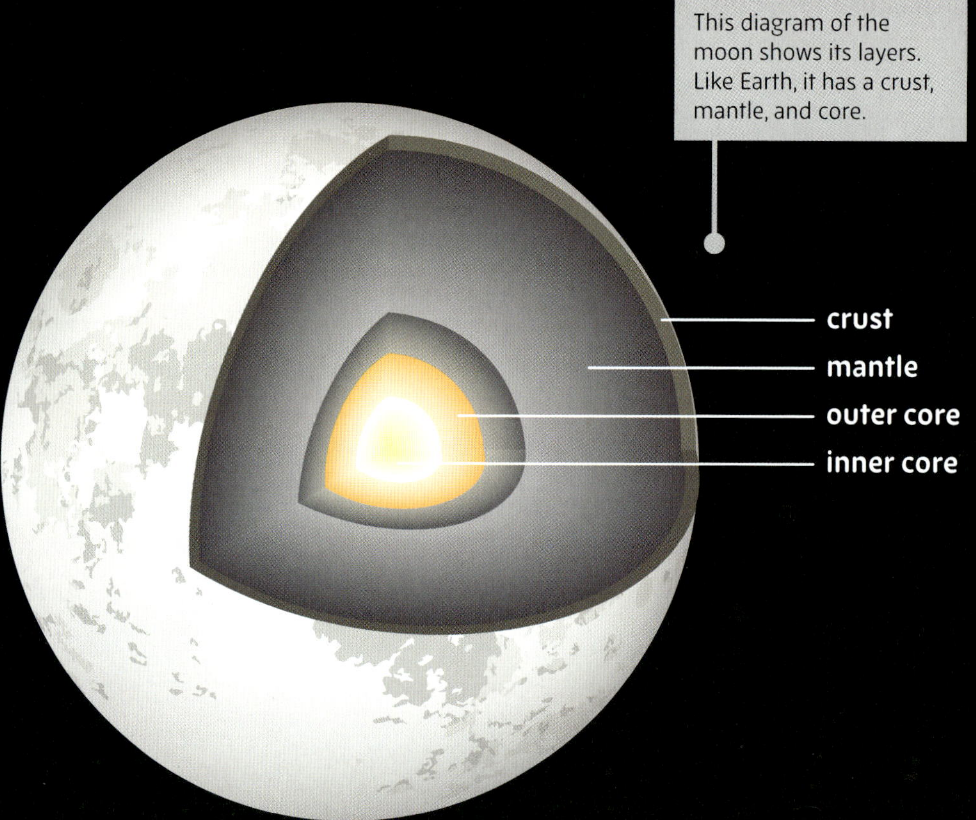

This diagram of the moon shows its layers. Like Earth, it has a crust, mantle, and core.

Seismic Studies

Scientists have learned about the moon by using the same technique used to study Earth's internal structure: measuring seismic waves and analyzing how they pass through the moon. Tremors called "moonquakes" take place on the moon, but they are very weak compared with earthquakes. Impacts from meteorites also cause tremors. Instruments placed on the moon's surface still record vibrations, providing crucial data.

Testing Moon Rocks

Rock samples brought back from the moon have been useful in many ways. The mix of elements found in moon rocks suggests that the moon was once heated to very high temperatures. Some types of elements are radioactive and decay over time, at a very regular rate. By taking precise measurements of the amount of these elements found in a rock sample, scientists can calculate how old the rock is. Tests on moon rocks have shown that some of them are 4.4 billion years old.

SPACE SCIENCE

The moon may have been created at the same time and from the same material as Earth, back in the early days of the solar system. It probably formed when a small planet collided with Earth, creating a huge cloud of rocky debris. This debris would have gradually clumped together to form the moon. Or it might have formed somewhere else and then been captured by Earth's gravity. Rocks brought back by the Apollo missions are slightly different from Earth rocks, so this supports the impact theory, but it is not yet completely proven.

This sample of moon rock was taken during the Apollo 17 mission to the moon. It provides useful information about the moon's history.

On the Surface

Early telescope users, such as Galileo, were able to see features on the moon's surface. There were dark, flat areas and jagged mountains, as well as deep canyons and circular craters. As telescopes improved, astronomers were able to make increasingly accurate maps of the moon's surface. When robotic probes started visiting the moon, we learned even more about it.

During Galileo's lifetime, most scientists believed that the moon was smooth, but the scientist discovered that it has mountains, craters, and other features, just like Earth.

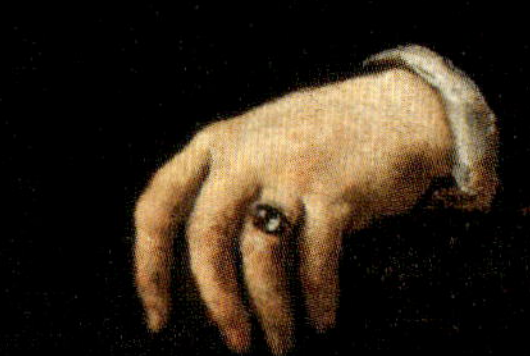

Flat and High

We now know that the moon's dark, flat areas (called maria, after the Latin word for "sea") were formed billions of years ago, when lava flowed across the moon's surface. They cover about 15 percent of the moon's surface and are much younger than other parts of the moon. In contrast, the brighter areas are known as highlands, or "terrae." NASA's Clementine spacecraft confirmed that the highlands are on average about 3.7 to 4.8 miles (6 to 7.7 km) higher than the maria.

Covered with Craters

The moon's highlands are rough, mountainous, and pockmarked with craters. The tiniest craters are microscopic, and the largest is about 180 miles (290 km) across. Evidence from the Apollo missions proved that they are caused by meteorite impacts. NASA estimates that 11 to 1,100 tons (10 to 1,000 mt) —that's the mass of about 5.5 cars— of dust collide with the moon every day. Around 100 pingpong-sized lumps of rock hit it every day, and about 33,000 meteorites each year!

Powder and Rubble

All of these features on the moon's surface are covered with a layer of fine powder and rubble anywhere from 3 to 60 feet (0.9 to 18 m) deep, called regolith. The regolith has been built up over billions of years by the debris of meteorite impacts. The meteorite impacts mix the soil from different areas of the moon's surface. When samples of lunar soil are analyzed, they often include rock fragments from hundreds of miles away.

SPACE SCIENCE

When NASA scientists examined the rocks brought back by the Apollo astronauts, some of the results looked rather familiar. The scientists realized that moon rocks had already been discovered, right here on Earth! They had been blasted from the moon's surface by impacts from meteoroids and had fallen as meteorites. At the time they were found, no one had realized that they came from the moon. Lunar meteorites are extremely rare—only around 370 have been discovered.

Astronaut Alan L. Bean is photographed here using a core sample tube to take soil samples from the moon's surface during the Apollo 12 mission.

Searching for Water

Water is necessary for all life on Earth, and so far Earth is the only place we know of where liquid water exists on the surface. The temperature on Earth is ideal for water, and our atmosphere keeps it from evaporating into space. However, scientists have discovered frozen water in other locations around the solar system. This is a key area of research, since a source of water would be a huge benefit to any human settlement planned for the moon or other planets.

Earth has an abundance of water—around two-thirds of our planet is covered with it. It has been essential for life.

Hidden Ice

Scientists have known for a long time that liquid water could not exist on the surface of the moon. However, in the 1960s they began to speculate that ice might exist there, hidden from the sun's light in deep craters. In 1978, a team of Soviet scientists published research that showed traces of water in rock samples brought back by Luna 24. Spacecraft such as Clementine and Lunar Prospector tried to find evidence of frozen water, but did not come up with anything conclusive.

Drier than a Desert

In 2009 the LCROSS probe impacted the moon's south pole, creating a plume of debris that was analyzed by scientists. The scientists discovered more water than they had expected, though the moon's surface is still drier than any desert on Earth. Many scientists theorized that water on the moon came from comet or meteorite impacts, but new research suggests that it might have formed on the moon after exposure to the solar wind.

SPACE SCIENCE

When some of Apollo's rock samples were first analyzed, tiny traces of water were found, but scientists assumed that this was as a result of contamination on Earth. However, the rocks were examined again in the 2000s with more sensitive tools. Scientists found that the pebbles contained small amounts of water, and they were able to prove that the water had not been a result of contamination on Earth.

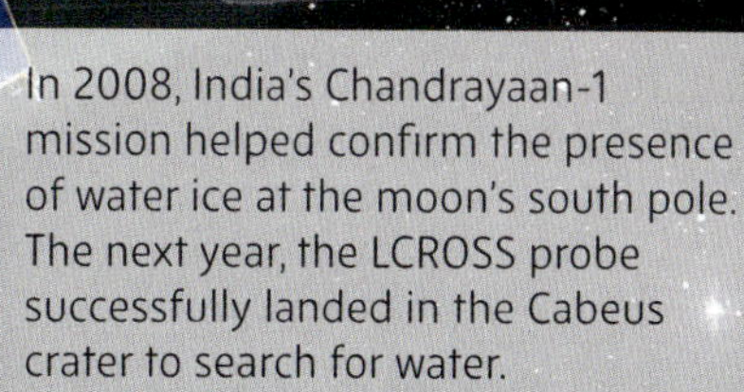

In 2008, India's Chandrayaan-1 mission helped confirm the presence of water ice at the moon's south pole. The next year, the LCROSS probe successfully landed in the Cabeus crater to search for water.

The International Space Station (ISS) orbits in the uppermost region of Earth's atmosphere, where it can survey our planet below.

No Protection

It is not just the moon's lack of oceans that sets it apart from Earth. The moon has virtually no atmosphere and no magnetic field. Both of these are crucial to life on Earth, so without their protection, life would be impossible on the moon.

Unlike Earth

The moon's atmosphere is extremely thin, about as dense as the outermost layers of Earth's atmosphere, where the ISS orbits. Unlike Earth's atmosphere, where the atoms and molecules constantly collide with each other, the moon's atmosphere is so thick that its atoms and molecules almost never collide. It is made up of a mixture of gases, including some that are not found in Earth's atmosphere.

A Magnetic Past

The moon contains very weak magnetism in its crust, but no powerful magnetic field like Earth has. Data gathered by the Apollo missions showed that it had a stronger magnetic field in the past. The rock samples they brought back showed evidence of being magnetized. This is usually caused by the rocks being heated and then cooled down in a magnetic field. The metallic particles in the rock "freeze" along the lines of the magnetic fields, leaving a permanent record.

A Liquid Core Long Ago

Scientists are puzzled by the moon's magnetic field: where did it come from, and why did it disappear? Unlike Earth's core, the moon's core is not magnetic. The magnetism of Earth is caused by convection currents in the liquid core, so if the moon's core is not magnetic, it probably has a solid core. Magnetized rocks suggest that the moon's core may have been liquid about 3.8 billion years ago.

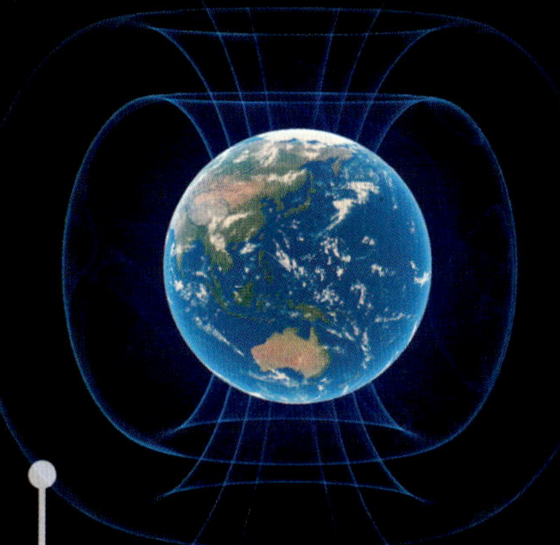

We have learned much about Earth's magnetic field but the moon's magnetism is more mysterious.

SPACE SCIENCE

The Apollo 17 astronauts set up a tool called the Lunar Atmospheric Composition Experiment (LACE) on the surface in 1972. LACE was able to detect tiny amounts of elements and compounds such as helium, argon, neon, methane, and carbon dioxide. Since then, researchers on Earth have been able to use telescopes to detect sodium and potassium atoms in the moon's atmosphere by making images of the atoms' glow as they are energized by the sun.

YOUR MISSION

The Apollo 13 mission to the moon almost ended in disaster in 1970 when an onboard fire damaged equipment. The team survived by utilizing their combined knowledge. Imagine you were in a similar situation on a mission—what would help you survive? Consider:

» What skills you would want in your team members
» What skills you have that would help you deal with the situation
» How STEM knowledge could help you survive

Chapter 5

OUR NEAREST NEIGHBOR

The moon is our closest neighbor in space, and we are able to see several of its features and behaviors in detail. One of these is the phases of the moon, as it appears to change shape over the course of a lunar cycle. Mercury and Venus have phases, too, but their orbits lie between Earth and the sun, so their phases cannot be seen with the naked eye. However, the moon's phases are easy to see.

This image shows the different phases of the moon. Full moon is shown center.

Lighting Up

Although the moon appears bright, it does not make its own light. Instead, it reflects light from the sun. Depending on where the moon is in its orbit of Earth, we see a different amount of it lit by the sun. For example, when the moon is on the opposite side of Earth from the sun, the sun's light illuminates its whole disc, and we see a full moon. When it is between Earth and the sun, its lit side is facing away from us, and it appears to disappear. When it is halfway between the two points, we see half of its lit face, giving it the appearance of a semicircle.

The Moon's Rotation

We always see the same side of the moon, but this does not mean the moon stays still. It rotates on its axis, just like Earth does, but it takes the same amount of time to rotate on its axis as it does to complete one orbit of Earth. This is called synchronous rotation, and many other moons in the solar system rotate in the same way.

This photograph of the moon shows the side that we do not see from Earth.

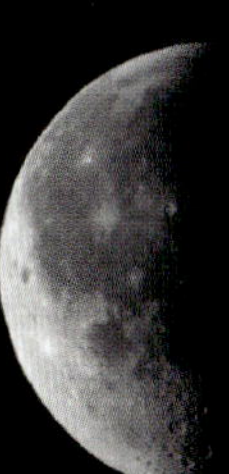

SPACE SCIENCE

In spite of the moon's synchronous rotation, over a period of time we are able to see a little more than half of its surface—about 59 percent, in fact. This is due to a phenomenon known as libration. The moon has a slight "wobble" as a result of small variations in its rotation speed, which are caused by its elliptical orbit. When the moon is slightly closer to Earth, it moves faster than when it is farther away, but its rotation speed stays the same, allowing us to see slightly beyond each edge of the moon as it speeds up and slows down in its orbit.

Creating Tides

The Earth has a huge influence on the moon and its force of gravity holds the moon in its orbit. However, the moon also influences conditions on Earth. It has its own gravity, and although it is weaker than Earth's, it still has an effect on our planet. When it pulls on Earth, it causes the side of it closest to the moon to "bulge" slightly. This effect is not really noticeable on land, but it is more dramatic at sea, and it is this that causes our tides.

High Tides

Some coastal regions get two high tides each day, and others have only one. The angle of the moon's orbit causes this difference. The moon does not orbit directly around Earth's equator, so at any given time the maximum "bulge" of the ocean is usually either above or below the equator. Some areas on Earth experience only one of the tidal bulges in a day.

When it is low tide, more of a beach, such as this one at Half Moon Bay in California, is revealed. At high tide, the water nears the shoreline and covers a greater area of sand once more.

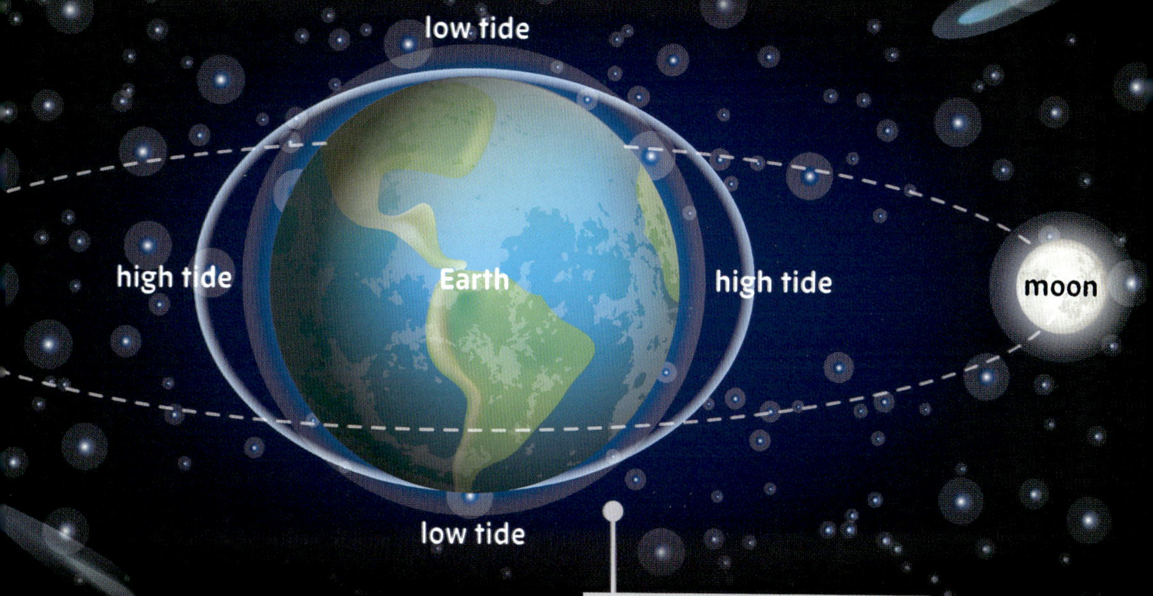

low tide

high tide

Earth

high tide

moon

low tide

The gravitational pull of the moon hauls up Earth's oceans into two bulges on opposite sides of the planet, as shown.

Lining Up

The moon orbits around Earth in the same direction that Earth rotates on its axis. This means that once the moon is in line with a particular point on Earth's surface, it takes nearly 25 hours to line up with that same point again. In an area that has two high tides each day, one high tide will come 12 hours and 25 minutes after the previous high tide.

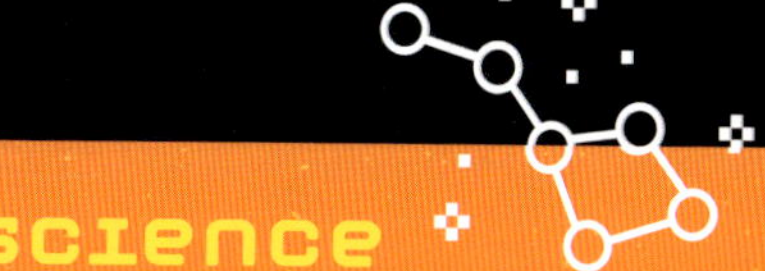

The sun's gravity also has an effect on tides, but since the sun is much farther away, its effect is not as strong as that of the moon's gravity. However, when the moon and sun are both in line with Earth, the force of their gravity is combined, and this creates a higher high tide than normal, called a spring tide. Midway between two spring tides we get a neap tide, where the sun and moon are pulling from different directions. The neap tide causes a smaller difference between high and low tides.

Full and Disappearing

The moon appears to disappear once a month, during the new moon phase. However, it can also nearly disappear for short periods at other times, when it is supposed to be full. This is called a lunar eclipse, and it happens when Earth moves directly between the sun and the moon, causing a shadow to cover its surface.

Lining up Perfectly

Although Earth passes between the moon and the sun once in each lunar cycle, we get a lunar eclipse only when they line up just right. This can happen from two to four times in a single year. Unlike a solar eclipse, which can be seen from only a relatively small area on Earth's surface, everyone on the night side of Earth can see a lunar eclipse.

An almost total eclipse of the moon took place in November 2021.

Moon Eclipses

The shadow that Earth casts on the moon has two parts: the umbra, or central region (where all of the sun's rays are blocked), and the penumbra, which is the outer region (where only some of the sun's rays are blocked). In a penumbral lunar eclipse, the moon passes through just the penumbra, and the visible effect on the moon is hardly noticeable. In a partial lunar eclipse, only part of the moon passes through the umbral shadow. These are easy to see, and the moon will look like it has a bite taken out of it. In a total lunar eclipse, the entire moon passes through the umbra. It appears to change color until it goes orange, red, or black.

A total solar eclipse can cause complete darkness in the middle of the day.

Lunar eclipses are impressive, but solar eclipses are even more amazing. During a total solar eclipse, the moon moves between the sun and Earth, and completely blocks the sun from some vantage points on Earth. The sun is about 400 times bigger in diameter than our moon, but it is also about 400 times farther away, so they appear almost exactly the same size in the sky. This makes the moon the perfect size to cover the sun.

YOUR MISSION

Your mission is to conduct safe and informative viewings of solar eclipses from Earth. In planning your mission, consider:

- Where would be best to see solar eclipses
- How they could be safely viewed
- What variations of solar eclipses might be seen and why

Chapter 6

ALWAYS MORE MISSIONS

The past decade has seen a surge of renewed interest in the moon. In 2009, NASA launched the Lunar Reconnaissance Orbiter (LRO), which has spent years making detailed maps in order to pave the way for astronauts to return to the moon. The data sent back by LRO can help identify possible landing sites by looking at the terrain, radiation, and usable resources within a specific location. LRO was joined in 2013 by the Lunar Atmosphere and Dust Environment Explorer (LADEE), which took readings of the moon's atmosphere and dust from orbit. The goal was to learn more about the behavior and effects of dust, which may affect exploration and astronomy on the moon.

This artist's image shows LADEE on its approach toward the moon.

Missions to the Moon

In 2013, the Chinese Chang'e 3 spacecraft became the first spacecraft since 1976 to soft-land on the moon. Its rover, named "Yutu," was unable to travel as far as was hoped, but it still managed to send back some useful data. The mission was planned as an intermediate step in China's moon exploration strategy. The first step was achieving moon orbit, which they did with Chang'e 1 and Chang'e 2. The third step is a sample return mission.

Asteroids Take Priority

There have been many proposals for sending astronauts back to the moon. NASA is currently working on its next crewed mission to the moon. In 2022, they sent the Artemis 1 mission on a loop around the moon and back to Earth. The Artemis 1 capsule was designed to take astronauts but this first mission was uncrewed.

SPACE SCIENCE

After early success, the Soviets pulled back from moon exploration in the 1970s. However, in 2023 Russia launched Luna 25, a robot lander designed to land near the moon's south pole. It successfully entered lunar orbit but technical problems led to the probe being destroyed in a crash landing on the lunar surface.

This illustration shows Russia's Luna 25 lander nearing the moon's surface. It is likely the lander crashed due to an onboard control failure.

This artist's illustration shows the SpaceX Crew Dragon spacecraft docking to the ISS. SpaceX is working with NASA to design, build, and operate vehicles that can safely transport materials and crew to and from the ISS.

Not Giving Up

NASA is encouraging private companies to take part in lunar exploration. In 2024, SpaceX launched a rocket carrying a moon lander made by another private company, Astrobiotic Technology. The mission did not succeed but it was the first attempt to land on the moon by a private company.

Why Do They Want to Go?

Why are private companies interested in going to the moon? The Apollo program came out of a desire to increase our scientific knowledge, and to beat the Soviet Union in the space race. The current crop of private entrepreneurs trying to develop spacecraft have different motives. Some might be interested in opening up the moon to tourism; others want to set up mining operations and exploit its mineral resources. Others see the moon as the obvious next step for human settlement.

Carrying Crew and Cargo

When the space shuttle program was terminated in 2011, NASA needed a new way to take crew and cargo back and forth to the ISS. They opened up cargo operations to private companies, believing that competition would lead to better prices. Two companies are now flying cargo missions to the ISS.

Difficult and Costly

Space exploration is difficult and expensive, even for a destination as close as the moon. National and international space agencies will always have a role to play. By working together with privately funded projects, they are beginning to revolutionize space exploration.

Guy Laliberté is a Canadian businessman who became the country's first space tourist in 2009. Space tourism is likely to become more popular as private investment in space science grows.

SPACE SCIENCE

The Google Lunar XPrize was announced in 2007 as a way of encouraging innovation in space exploration. The challenge was simple: land a robot on the moon, make it travel more than 1,640 feet (500 m), and send back high-definition images and video. The first team to accomplish the mission would win $20 million, and the second-place prize was $5 million. Other prizes were available to rovers that completed additional tasks. Entry was only available to teams that received fewer than 10 percent of their funding from government sources. The competition was open until 2018 when the unclaimed cash prizes were withdrawn.

A Good Idea

Astronauts live on the ISS for months at a time. Could they live just as easily on the moon? For a long time, moon bases were a topic for science fiction, and not a realistic project. It is easy, however, to see why the idea is so attractive. The moon has valuable mineral resources, and it is also a useful place for experiments. Its lack of a thick atmosphere would make it an ideal site for telescopes, and scientists could carry out experiments in its low gravity.

Not Without Problems

However, setting up a moon base would be challenging. To support a human population, we would need to recreate conditions similar to Earth. Human colonists would need air to breathe, water to drink, and food to eat. They would need to be protected from extreme temperatures, solar radiation, and the near-vacuum on the surface.

Benefits of the Moon

The moon has several advantages over other possible destinations, such as Mars. For one thing, it is very close. It took Apollo 11 about three days to reach the moon, but to get to Mars would take about six months. This means that transporting cargo and crew back and forth to the moon will be much easier. The discovery of water ice on the moon is also a positive sign. Astronauts could use this for drinking, as well as for making rocket fuel and air. The oxygen locked in the moon's soil could be harvested using heat and electricity to provide breathable air for the colonists.

A moon base may currently look and sound like the stuff of science fiction, but it could become a reality that will change the way we explore space.

Space Science

Human bodies are not designed to cope without gravity. Astronauts who have spent several months on the ISS often need to be carried away on stretchers once they land back on Earth. This is because their muscles do not have to work as hard when they are weightless in space. Their muscles lose mass, and so do their bones. Astronauts on the ISS follow a carefully designed fitness program to keep from losing too much muscle and bone mass. Any long-term residents of the moon's lower gravity would need to do the same.

Your Mission

It is your mission to invent technology that can help stop loss of muscle mass in space. In your work, consider:

- The materials you would use to make the technology
- The practical use of the technology in spacecraft, where space and movement is limited
- How any equipment could be stored to be space-efficient
- How you would make the technology desirable for use by astronauts in space
- How you would test a prototype

FUTURE MISSIONS

The future of space exploration will depend on our ability to develop new technologies. And the outlook on that front is very positive—it is astonishing to think that a modern smartphone has more computing power than the spacecraft that took Neil Armstrong, Michael Collins, and Buzz Aldrin to the moon!

New Technology

NASA and other space agencies are working on concepts and prototypes for a variety of new technologies. For example, there are scientists working on different systems of propulsion to make transporting astronauts and cargo cheaper and easier. Improved, more precise guidance and landing systems will make entering orbit and landing safer. It currently costs about $50,000 to send one pound of material to the moon, but new, lightweight materials could make spacecraft lighter, and therefore cheaper to launch.

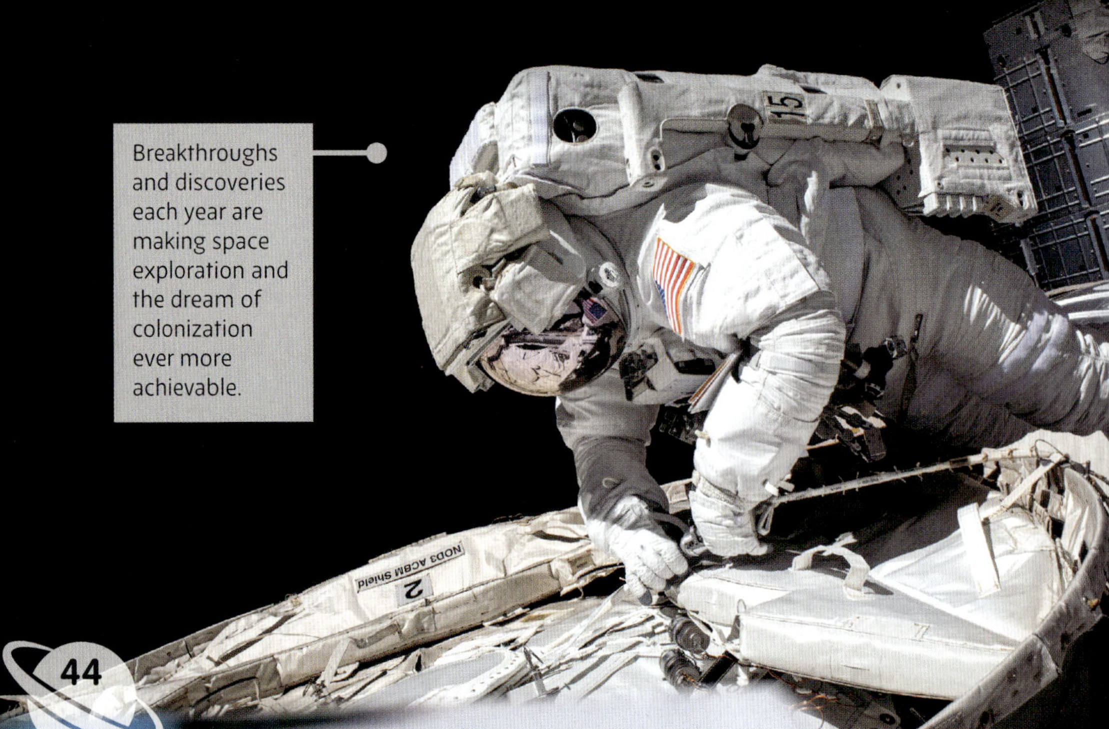

Breakthroughs and discoveries each year are making space exploration and the dream of colonization ever more achievable.

Living on Other Worlds

However, the spacecraft that will take astronauts to the moon is only one piece of the puzzle. Scientists are also working on more efficient ways to provide low-cost power for long trips as well as for settlements. Improvements to space suits will allow astronauts to explore and carry out research outside their base. Research continues into life-support systems that will allow humans to live on other worlds.

Living on the Moon

One promising new technology is the use of inflatable habitats to house moon colonists. NASA has tested a type of inflatable dwelling, similar to a carnival moonwalk, in the harsh conditions of Antarctica. If successful, these units would provide living space that could be insulated, heated, and pressurized. It would be fairly lightweight, so transporting it to the moon would not be difficult. It can also be taken down and reused multiple times.

YOUR FUTURE MISSION

Perhaps this book has inspired you to find out more about our Earth, moon, and space. Maybe, one day, you'll even carve out a career in space science and make it your mission to explore the mysteries of the universe and unlock its secrets.

GLOSSARY

asteroid a small, rocky body that orbits the sun

atmosphere the layer of gases surrounding a planet or moon

atoms the smallest possible units of a chemical element. Atoms are the basis of all matter in the universe

aurora a glow in the upper atmosphere caused when particles from the sun interfere with Earth's magnetic field

axis an imaginary line through the center of a planet, around which it rotates

compounds substances made up of two or more different elements that are bonded together

convection a way of transferring heat in a liquid or gas, when warmer, less dense material moves upward and is replaced by cooler, denser material

core the center of something

craters hollow areas, like the inside of a bowl, created when an object crashes into a planet or other large object

crust the hard outer shell of something

elements substances that cannot be separated into simpler substances

equator an imaginary line around the center of a planet or moon, halfway between its two poles

gravity the force that pulls all objects toward each other

lander a spacecraft designed to land on the surface of a planet or other object and send back data

magnetic field the space around a magnet in which a magnetic force is active

magnetosphere the region surrounding a planet or other object in which its magnetic field is always the dominant magnetic field

mantle the layer of Earth that lies between the crust and the core

mass a measure of how much matter is in an object

meteorite a lump of stone or metal from meteors that have landed on Earth

orbit the curved path that one body in space takes around another, such as a moon orbiting a planet

phase the apparent change in the shape of the moon, Venus, or Mercury, as seen from Earth as they move in their orbits

probes instruments or tools used to explore something that cannot be observed directly

radiation waves of energy sent out by sources of heat or light, such as the sun. Radiation can be harmful to living things

rotates spins around a central axis

rovers robotic vehicles designed to travel across the surface of a planet or moon and collect data

seismic waves waves of energy generated by an earthquake or other event that traveled within Earth or along its surface

solar eclipse a phenomenon that occurs when the moon travels directly between Earth and the sun, blocking its light

solar wind a flow of charged particles that travels out from the sun into the solar system

tectonic plates the segments of Earth's crust that move around in relation to one another

tides the regular change in the height of the surface of oceans and other bodies of water, caused by the pull of the moon's gravity

universe all matter and energy that exists

BOOKS

Barr, Catherine. *Voyage Through the Solar System* (Space Voyage). Rosen Publishing Group, 2022.

National Geographic Kids. *Space Encyclopedia: A Tour of Our Solar System and Beyond*. National Geographic Kids, 2020.

Reagan, Lisa. *Our Solar System* (Fact Frenzy). Rosen Publishing Group, 2021.

WEBSITES

Discover more about our amazing planet at:
kids.britannica.com/students/article/Earth/274103

Find out more about Earth's nearest neighbor, the moon, at:
kids.britannica.com/students/article/Moon/275930

Learn more fascinating facts about Earth and the moon at:
www.nationalgeographic.co.uk/search?q=earth+and+the+moon

Publisher's note to educators and parents:
All the websites featured above have been carefully reviewed to ensure that they are suitable for students. However, many websites change often, and we cannot guarantee that a site's future contents will continue to meet our high standards of educational value. Please be advised that students should be closely monitored whenever they access the Internet.

INDEX

ABOUT THE AUTHOR

Sarah Eason has written many children's books and has a particular interest in space science. She has found researching and writing this book fascinating and hopes that it helps readers better understand the mysteries of space and maybe make it their mission to become a future space explorer.